KEITH PIRT COLOUR PORTFOLIO

BRITISH RAILWAYS DIESELS

Keith R. Pirt

with contributions from Hugh Ballantyne and Roger Griffiths

BOOK LAW PUBLICATIONS

1

'Deltic' 55008 THE GREEN HOWARDS climbs past Saltersford with a York-King's Cross express in October 1980. *(BLP - D111)*

First published in the United Kingdom by Book Law Publications 2006
382 Carlton Hill, Nottingham, NG4 1JA
Printed and bound by The Amadeus Press, Cleckheaton, West Yorkshire.

Introduction

The implementation of the British Railways Modernisation Plan in 1955 resulted in the introduction of numerous pilot classes of main line diesel locomotives. These new diesels, which came into service from late 1957 onwards, came a little bit too early and the dedicated servicing and maintenance facilities needed to keep them going was not then in place and would not be for a few years. The original scheme was to assess these classes for suitable designs for mass production but the requirement of the quick elimination of steam motive power overruled those plans.

Originally the new diesel locomotives were painted in Brunswick green livery, although the need for visibility resulted in yellow painted ends within a few years. When steam finally disappeared in 1968 a new, uninspiring, corporate blue livery began to replace the green. After a decade of the monotonous blue, some livery variations, many with large logos, eventually emerged.

Although steam was my priority with photography, a few new diesels were recorded and now, with hindsight, more should have been recorded. Pictures were taken up to 1987 of nose-ended diesel locomotive classes, mainly in corporate liveries. However, privatisation and sectorisation killed my interest especially when the smaller older types were scrapped and new larger cab-ended classes took over. This book covers thirty years of a selection of my main line diesel photographs. There are only a few shunters and a single multiple unit train is represented - a Western Region Pullman.

K.R.Pirt, Clowne, November 2004.

The editorial team would like to thank Hugh Ballantyne and Roger Griffiths for contributing some of the photographic material found herein. It will be noted that these two gentlemen are responsible for the diesel-hydraulic illustrations which were somewhat lacking in Keith's portfolio. On the other hand the number of Deltic illustrations is all down to KRP. No doubt he had something of a soft spot for those locomotives when they ran the ECML expresses - or maybe it was the ECML for which he had the soft spot. Anyway, enjoy these classic views which hopefully will bring back many memories to you all.

There is no apparent order to the presentation of the illustrations, either on a geographical, regional, date, or class order. The reason being is that we wanted, like Keith Pirt intended, to present a portfolio of pictures which can be both enjoyed and studied with a surprise element on the turning of each page.

Crewe based EE Type 4 D370 heads a Llandudno bound train between Abergele and Colwyn Bay on the North Wales coast line in July 1963. Note the centrally situated headcode box which became standard for the last fifty-odd engines; this type of display had superseded the split box display which had been introduced in the latter months of 1960. Another feature which was eventually added to all the class was the rectangular yellow warning panel, which in turn gave way to the whole ends of the locomotives being painted yellow. The London Midland based EE Type 4's had a good innings on the West Coast Main Line being the only available main line diesels on the newly titled 'Western Lines' capable enough to at least equal the Stanier Pacific performances on the named expresses of the day. However, in 1966 when the 25kV overhead electrification finally reached Euston these diesels were only used on the Anglo-Scottish expresses north of Crewe and when the fifty EE Type 4 Co-Co's arrived en masse in 1968, their days as first choice motive power was over. The last of the EE Type 4's, D399, was not delivered from Vulcan Foundry until September 1962 and along with the last fifteen of the class it went to the NE Region working secondary expresses, their chances of working the premier express trains on the ECML having long gone with the advent of the EE Type 5's. *(BLP - D19)*

D1 SCAFELL PIKE, the first of the hugely successful 'Peak' class diesel-electrics. This July 1970 view, captured at Toton depot, shows the locomotive attached to a 'brake tender' because by now the ten original 'Peaks', classified as Class 44 under TOPS, were all relegated to freight service and worked solely from the East Midlands shed. Except for the disc type headcode, the ten members of Class 44 were outwardly similar in many respects to the Class 45 and 46 locomotives which carried the more conventional box-like route indicators. Inwardly the newer locomotive from D11 to D193 were equipped with 2,500 horsepower Sulzer diesel engines against the 2,300 h.p. Sulzers of those first ten. When it first entered service in the summer of 1959, D1 was allocated, along with the other nine original 'Peaks' to the West Coast Main Line and worked the passenger services from Camden, Crewe, Edge Hill, Longsight and Carlisle Upperby depots for a short time until the English Electric Type 4 entered service in some numbers. *(BLP - D59)*

It is July 1961, the location is just north of Hadley Wood tunnel, the weather is hot and the sun is just right. Expecting ECML Pacifics to be the main fare for the afternoon, KRP caught on film this Brush Type 2, D5644, in between the steam hauled main line trains. Although not noted as such, the train was probably one of the Cambridge workings from King's Cross, a service which at that time was fully utilising these Type 2s. Not yet a year old, D5644 was one of the many of its class allocated to the then newly opened Finsbury Park diesel depot. When BR renumbered its diesel locomotive fleet under the TOPS scheme, D5644 became Class 31 219. Note the lack of the yellow warning panel. *(BLP - D137)*

Darnall based Brush Type 2 D5691 approaches Millhouses with a Sheffield (Midland) to Manchester (Central) train in June 1965. The green liveried Type 2's became one of the success stories of the diesel age and many of the original 263 strong class are still working in 2004/5. The type, starting with D5500, first appeared in October 1957 with the first twenty going to work the former Great Eastern lines from Stratford shed and of the first two hundred locomotives approximately sixty worked the former Great Northern lines out of King's Cross, fifteen worked from Sheffield Darnall with the other one hundred and twenty-five working on the old GE from Ipswich, Norwich and Stratford. Of the final sixty-three, starting with D5800 which was delivered in June 1961, the first four went to the GE lines whilst the remainder D5804 to D5862 all went to Darnall. The Sheffield based engines found themselves on all types of work from semi-fast passenger trains, such as this, to coal train haulage, the latter often in tandem to provide the extra braking power required to keep these trains in check. The Darnall fleet moved to the newly opened depot at Tinsley yard in April 1964 and from there they would spend many weeks working from the sub depots and stabling points in the coalfields such as Rotherwood, Shirebrook, Wath and Worksop. *(BLP - D33)*

7

March based Brush Type 2 D5576, passes the newly excavated dive-under at Retford (Thrumpton) in October 1964 with westbound coal empties from Whitemoor yard. This particular coal train working was a throwback to the pre-Grouping days when Great Eastern 0-6-0's would work up from March with trains of empty wagons to the coal producing areas in Nottinghamshire, South Yorkshire and Derbyshire, mostly using the LD&ECR route before 1923. During LNER days and indeed in BR days the coal hungry counties of Cambridgeshire, Essex, Norfolk and Suffolk would be catered for by these long distance hauls which entered the coalfield via various routes including this one over the old GCR. The dive-under here was excavated to take the former GC route beneath the ECML and do away with the flat crossing which had served the two lines since 1852. The cost of the new works was just over £1 million and the reason for so much expenditure was not merely from a safety point of view but more from an operational one because the newly constructed base load power stations in the Trent valley required vast amounts of coal and this was to be catered for using 'merry-go-round' air-braked coal trains which would not only speed up the delivery of the coal but would bring a great efficiency in the fact that they could be unloaded at the power station in just over an hour without the need to uncouple either the hauling locomotive or any portion of the train. Over a thousand tons would be carried on each train and as many as twenty-four trains a day would serve each of the two stations, Cottam and West Burton. A total of 330,000 cubic yards of excavation was required for the new dive-under which was just under a mile long. Work started in November 1963 and the completion date was mid-June 1965. In the centre background is the former Great Northern Railway Retford engine shed, the exGreat Central shed at Thrumpton, just to the east of the ECML, was closed priot to the diveunder becoming operational. *(BLP - D161)*

Three years into its British Railways loan period, the 'Deltic' prototype climbs Gamston curve with an afternoon Leeds to King's Cross express in October 1958. Initially this locomotive was to carry the designation DP1 (an English Electric locomotive similar in looks to the production 'Deltics' but internally different, joined the BR fleet 'on loan' in May 1962 and was numbered DP2) but it was, fortuitously, named DELTIC instead. Built at the English Electric Dick Kerr works in Preston, the blue 'Deltic' went to London Midland Region at first and it was tried out on most of the express passenger trains which plied the West Coast Main Line, especially the *MERSEYSIDE EXPRESS*. The LMR did not show too much interest in the Deltic because electrification of the Euston to Liverpool and Manchester routes was well into the planning stage by December 1955 and so eventually it made its debut on the ECML and the rest of course is history. *(BLP - D22)*

The tranquillity of the river bank is about to be shattered as the blue 'Deltic' approaches the River Idle bridge at Ordsall with a Down express in November 1960. This engine was allocated to Hornsey depot in north London during its ECML years of BR 'service' and this particular November would be its last thundering up and down the main line. During the following March it was retired as the first four of the eventual twenty-two production models began their work. Luckily the Science Museum took over custody of this revolutionary locomotive and still today it makes a very impressive sight at the National Railway Museum. *(BLP - D51)*

'Peak' D50 is framed in the road bridge at Millhouses on a St Pancras express, IM88 in June 1964. This engine became Class 45 under TOPS and was renumbered to 45040 in January 1975. In May 1965 this Derby based but Crewe built 'Peak' was named THE KING'S SHROPSHIRE LIGHT INFANTRY. It later moved to Tinsley depot and was based there when withdrawal came in July 1987. It gained a new lease of life when it became a Departmental locomotive, numbered 97412. *(BLP - D12)*

Only days old, the second production Deltic, D9001 looking splendid in its two tone green livery, leaves Retford for King's Cross with the morning train from Leeds in February 1961. Unusually the central headcode display is blank. *(BLP - D4)*

(opposite) Open days at Staveley Barrow Hill engine shed became a regular event after the demise of steam traction and today they continue to draw in the crowds for some of the best shows every year. In September 1971 the yard was graced with the presence of HS 4000 KESTREL, a unique experimental diesel-elctric locomotive which spent much of its three years 'on loan' to British Railways working coal trains from North Midland collieries to power stations. Built by Brush, and on loan from January 1968 to January 1971, the locomotive did not seem to impress the relevant authorities and it was stored at the Loughborough works of its manufacturer for some time before being sold to the Soviet Union where it was used for research until 1988. On this September day it had been brought to the show especially and looks attractive in its yellow and brown livery, all of which was quite a contrast to the preserved Peppercorn A2 No.532 BLUE PETER in the background. *(BLP - D37)*

North British Locomotive Co. built Type 2 diesel-electric D6102 stands outside the paint shop at Doncaster works in September 1958 after delivery from Glasgow. D6102 was allocated to Hornsey depot during the following December to work passenger trains on the southern section of the ECML alongside nine others of the class. NBL built a total of fifty-eight of these particular locomotives which with their MAN engines were destined to be one of the failures of the 1955 BR Modernisation plan. Originally rated at 1,100 horsepower, the whole class suffered numerous mechanical problems and by February 1960 the Hornsey based locomotives were stored unserviceable. Twenty of the class were given new, more powerful (1,350 h.p.) Paxman engines during the mid-1960s and D6102 was one of those chosen to be fitted with the new prime mover. Not that the new power plant made any difference because unreliability dogged the whole class throughout their somewhat short lives. In December 1967 the first withdrawals had taken place with nearly half the class, now all based in Scotland, condemned in that month. This featured locomotive was condemned in October 1971 and was cut up at BR's Glasgow works in August 1972 whilst many of its classmates went to private scrap merchants. Under the TOPS system, BR classified these locomotives as Class 21 but the twenty which were re-engined became Class 29. *(BLP - D52)*

North British Locomotive Co. 1960 built Type 2 Bo-Bo D6152, in green livery, departs Stonehaven station with an Aberdeen Down local in May 1965 with more than half its life already expired. As mentioned opposite, the first ten went to Hornsey, whilst the following ten went to Stratford and the balance were allocated to Ipswich depot. Later the Scottish Region got its own delivery of new Type 2's from the NBL., D6138 to D6157. Once the class was assembled in Scotland they resided basically at two depots - Eastfield and Kittybrewster. Like the 'Baby Deltics' they were destined to be amongst the less successful diesels of those early years and reliability was not a word to be associated with this class. In an effort to give the design more power and reliability, twenty of the former ER based locomotives were re-engined with a more powerful prime mover between 1963 and 1967. By mid 1967, all but one of the original Scotland based locomotives had been stored and by the end of the year were withdrawn. The other unaltered engines soon followed and even the refurbished locomotives had all been withdrawn by December 1971. The NBL diesel electric Type 2 was best forgotten along with their diesel hydraulic cousins which roamed the Western Region for a similar period of time. *(BLP - D3)*

The first ten English Electric Type 4 diesels all came into traffic during 1958 and were allocated to the Eastern Region with D200 and D202-D205 going to Stratford shed for Great Eastern line workings, and D201 with D206-D209 to Hornsey shed for East Coast Main Line workings. However, all ten often worked from either shed. D209 was the last of that initial batch and entered BR service in September. The following month, whilst working the *MASTER CUTLER* Pullman service between Sheffield (Victoria) and King's Cross, the engine had need to top up the water tank feeding its steam heating boiler and it was necessary to use water columns, as here outside Sheffield (Victoria) station. One wonders how much water was sometimes spilt inside the locomotive during these somewhat precarious filling operations. Steam heating of coaching stock was still prevalent at this early stage of BR modernisation and many of the early main line diesels were fitted with water scoops which enabled them to pick-up water from troughs. Note that headcode discs were normal for these early diesels. *(BLP - D24)*

EE Type 4 D201 passes the 100 milepost at Stoke summit with a heavy Newcastle to King's Cross express on a lovely sunny day in June 1960. Of the eventual two hundred locomotives in this class, only eighty-odd had been delivered by this date and most of those were working on the ECML from Finsbury Park, York, Gateshead and Haymarket depots. The EE Type 5, the 'Deltics' had yet to appear and so these 133 ton monsters were, for a short period, the preferred motive power for the ECML expresses. The Gresley and Peppercorn Pacifics still had plenty of work on the same trains but their days were numbered. *(BLP - D21)*

Already one year old and still looking immaculate in its two tone green livery, D9007 PINZA, nears Gamston box with the Up *NORTHUMBRIAN* express for King's Cross in June 1962. *(BLP - D5)*

(opposite) One of the least successful classes of the Modernisation Plan diesels was the English Electric Type 2 Bo-Bo's, the so-called 'Baby Deltics'. These locomotives had a frontal appearance of the EE Type 4's but with a shorter nose and a much shorter body which contained a single Deltic engine. They were designed to work short distance stopping trains on the southern end of the ECML into King's Cross and all ten were initially allocated to Hornsey shed but eventually went to Finsbury Park depot when that place was opened for business. D5904 was one of the first two put into traffic in April 1961 and by June the rest of the class were working. In August 1961 D5904, in the two-tone green livery, is just south of Hatfield with an Up local train for King's Cross. Within months the whole class were showing signs of unreliability and this manifested itself in temporary withdrawal and then storage at Stratford. Eventually Vulcan Foundry called them all back in for remedial work and refurbishment. Put back into traffic, they never lived up to expectation and in September 1968 the first condemnation took place when D5906 was withdrawn. Another seven succumbed over the next year but the final two in traffic, D5905 and D5909 lasted until early 1971. All except one were cut up by private contractors, most of them only eight years old. The exception was D5901 which was put into Departmental Stock. They would have become Class 23 under the TOPS scheme but did not last long enough to be renumbered. The early 1960's might have been a bad time for steam locomotives but the latter years of that decade were bad ones for the pioneer diesel designs. *(BLP - D6)*

The last member of the class put into traffic, Haymarket based D9021 has acquired cab roof horns and large yellow warning panels but it is still unnamed as it nears Little Ponton, south of Grantham, with 1A03, an Edinburgh to King's Cross express, in June 1962. This engine was late arriving on the ECML because the LMR had seconded it for a few weeks, after its departure from Vulcan Foundry, so that it could be tested on the Styal line with the 25kV electric locomotives which were themselves still being delivered. What the tests concluded I have no idea but the appearance of this engine on the Styal line for a couple of weeks must have had a few enthusiasts scratching their heads at the time (the Deltic's were no strangers to Manchester as they all passed through the city on their delivery runs to Doncaster but they did not use the lines through the southern suburbs). *(BLP - D10)*

What a difference a year makes. D9013 THE BLACK WATCH has charge of the Up *NORTHUMBRIAN* near Gamston signal box in June 1963. Compare the external appearance of this Haymarket engine with that of the Finsbury Park based D9007 in the previous illustration with the same train, at the same location. Note also the acquisition of the large yellow warning panel. *(BLP - D29)*

Haymarket's D9019 races south near Barrowby Road Junction box, Grantham with the Up *TEES-TYNE PULLMAN* in April 1962. This was the last 'Deltic' to acquire a name and it proudly became ROYAL HIGHLAND FUSILIER in September 1965. *(BLP - D14)*

(opposite) The BR 1955 Modernisation plan was, some might say, a 'stab in the dark' and a waste of money. Certainly it was radical and perhaps the way it was implemented was a little naive. That so many different types of diesel locomotives were ordered from so many outside firms seems, with hindsight, utterly ridiculous but having been given the order to modernise the railway system of Britain, the British Transport Commission went about its task with a gusto that was almost reckless. We are all aware of the 'failed' types and the Metropolitan-Vickers Co-Bo could well be a candidate to head the list of least successful. The twenty strong class started out with something of a handicap in that they had the most unusual bogie configuration - Co-Bo - whereby the six-wheel bogie was fitted beneath the engine compartment whilst the four-wheel bogie supported the generator end of the locomotive. This is the sole survivor, S15705 at Derby works in the early 1970's when it was being used by the Research and Technical Centre for haulage of their special trains. Starting life in December 1958 as D5705, this now preserved locomotive was put into service on the former Midland Lines where it was used in multiple with other Co-Bos on the nocturnal *CONDOR* fast goods services between London and Glasgow. Besides the freight duties, the class were used on a variety of main line passenger services, again usually in multiple, on trains to Manchester (Central). Beset with problems from their Crossley two-stroke engines, the whole class was put into store at various sites during the early months of 1961. A year later, after remedial work by the makers at the former Great Central carriage works in Dukinfield, they were put back into service but were relegated to secondary duties on the ex Furness Railway lines, based at Barrow. After such an inglorious start, being far from 'standard' and having the only two stroke engines then put to railway traction use, it was obvious that these 'oddballs' were destined for an early demise so that it was no surprise when the last examples of what were to become Class 28, were condemned in September 1968. *(BLP - D126)*

Brush Type 4 D1547 in the distinctive two tone green livery bestowed on this class, leaves Sheffield (Midland) station and is passing Farm grounds with an inter-regional express bound for the West Country in July 1966. The diveunder here, constructed by the Midland Railway, was still being used and although some colour light signalling was in situ, semaphore signals controlled much of the traffic. Sheffield's Darnall depot was the recipient of thirty-six new Brush Type 4's between August 1963 and March 1964 but D1547 was not one of them, its first depot of allocation being Finsbury Park. The Darnall Brush 4's all moved to the newly opened Tinsley depot in April 1964 and over the next twelve months were joined there by another seventy-odd of their ilk, giving Tinsley the largest allocation of the 512 strong class. *(BLP - D2)*

'Peak' D78, one of the December 1960 Crewe built examples, heads a Leeds (City) to St.Pancras express near Sheffield Millhouses in September 1964. The Derby based locomotive has a light load and would have no trouble getting this train to its destination on time. Extremely reliable, the 'Peaks' could be found all over the Midland lines besides the ECML and the West of England main line of the WR. They were at home on express passenger trains, fitted freights and mineral workings. Their 138-ton weight barred them from many routes and the extremely long 1Co-Co1 bogies were sometimes a handicap but otherwise they certainly repaid their investment. I have one question which a reader might be able to answer for me - why did BR build just 193 'Peaks', why not 200 or 190 perhaps? *(BLP - D26)*

One of the three Western Region blue Pullman sets descends Hatton bank on a Wolverhampton to Paddington working in June 1962. Although outwardly they had something of a permanence about them, these revolutionary trains were intended as a 1960's stop-gap to tempt businessmen from the airlines and the motorways. The Western Region had three eight-car units each of which had 1st and 2nd Class accommodation. The WR utilised one unit on the London to Cardiff route, one unit on the Paddington to Wolverhampton route with one unit spare to cover for failures and maintenance. The London Midland Region had two six-car units both of which were 1st Class only. One unit was used Monday to Friday only on the early morning non-stop Manchester (Central) to London (St Pancras) service, returning to Manchester in the evening. Whilst in London awaiting its return working, that unit was put to work on the St Pancras to Nottingham return service. Meanwhile, the spare unit languished in Reddish depot until the following morning when it then took on the London service. When the Manchester (Piccadilly) to London (Euston) electrification was completed in 1966, the diesel powered Midland Pullman service was withdrawn and the two six-car sets sent to the Western. However, utilisation of the five units was no better and the fact that so much expensive equipment could be out of service for half of its life, simply because of under utilisation seems to be wasteful at least and virtually criminal in the extreme but then, that was BR in the 1960's. *(BLP - D42)*

Western Region diesel-hydraulic 'Warship' Class 42 No.827 KELLY arrives at Gillingham station with the 8.50 a.m. Exeter (St Davids) to Waterloo train on 29th August 1970. Coincidental with regional boundary changes, these Type 4s took over the majority of the Waterloo-Exeter passenger services in August 1964 from the Southern Region 'West Country/Battle of Britain' and 'Merchant Navy' Pacifics and performed admirably until they in turn handed over those duties to the Class 33 diesel-electric's in October 1972. The latter locomotives which were rated as Type 3 were did not perform anywhere near as well as the 'Warships' but they were the only locomotives available to the Southern at that time. *Hugh Ballantyne.*

All the Gateshead and Haymarket based 'Deltics' were named after British Army regiments, the Gateshead engines after English regiments and the Haymarket locomotives, naturally after Scottish regiments. D9006 was to become THE FIFE AND FORFAR YEOMANRY in December 1964 but that was some time off from this July 1961 view of it heading the Up *FLYING SCOTSMAN* at Ganwick. *(BLP - D23)*

(opposite) Amongst the numerous diesel types which appeared during the 1960's, one of the most unusual was the Class 13 'Master and Slave' units built in 1965 for working the hump at the then new Tinsley marshalling yard. Three 'locomotives' in all were constructed at Darlington utilising six BR 350 h.p. diesel-electric 0-6-0 shunters. The concept of the 'master and slave' or 'cow and calf' locomotive was first used by the railroads of the United States and BR decided that three such units would be ideal for the Sheffield yard. We are looking at 13002 alongside the fuelling bay at Tinsley diesel depot, 9th April 1978. Nearest the camera is the 'master' (exD4187) which is permanently coupled to the cabless 'slave' (exD3697). One driver had control of both power units, which in essence became one locomotive. The last of the trio to come into traffic, in July 1965, 13002 was originally numbered D4502, the other two D4500 and D4501 entered traffic during the previous May and June respectively. The reason for having three such units at Tinsley was to have one working the hump, one on stand-by or at times of excessive traffic working a separate rake of wagons over the hump, and one in maintenance. During the 1950's and 60's BR spent vast amounts of money creating large new marshalling yards to replace many of the older smaller yards. Some of the existing yards were updated and refurbished. However, the decline in freight traffic which had been taking place since Nationalisation, was never stemmed and the marshalling yards never did get used to their full potential. Tinsley suffered as much as any other yard and in June 1981 No.13002, was withdrawn leaving the other units to carry on until January 1985 when they too were condemned. Tinsley yard closed shortly afterwards and after a period of years when it was used for the storage of dozens of redundant diesel locomotives, it was lifted. *Hugh Ballantyne.*

D1068 WESTERN RELIANCE stands outside Canton depot in Cardiff , October 1975. This locomotive still had another year of service in front of it before withdrawal. One of the Crewe built examples, D1068 entered traffic in July 1963 working from Old Oak Common depot. By the time of its demise in October 1976 it had spent its last ten years working from Laira depot in Plymouth. The last of the 'Westerns', D1010, D1013, D1023 and D1048 were all withdrawn at the end of February 1977 and with that event came the end of the Western Region's diesel-hydraulic empire which had been planned some twenty-odd years previously during the days when Swindon was allowed to make its own way in the world. *Roger Griffiths*.

Virtually brand new 'Peak' D192, the penultimate member of the class, passes Ordsall with the Up *TEES-TYNE PULLMAN* in March 1963. This was one of the 'Peaks' fitted with Brush electrical equipment and which became Class 46 under the TOPS coding. It was renumbered to 46055 in February 1974. Spending most of its life allocated to Gateshead depot this locomotive would often work into the Western Region on inter-regional trains, getting as far south as Plymouth. Withdrawn in May 1981, it was reinstated during January 1982 but finally succumbed in October of that year and was cut up at Swindon works in November 1984. *(BLP - D28)*

Looking every bit its 3,300 h.p., D9010 THE KINGS OWN SCOTTISH BORDERER, now in blue livery, climbs Cockburnspath bank with an Edinburgh to King's Cross express in May 1968. *(BLP - D20)*

(opposite) Just a few weeks old, York based EE Vulcan Foundry built D354 heads the 7.20 a.m. Saltburn to King's Cross express just south of Hatfield in August 1961. It was usual for all the new Eastern and North Eastern Region based diesel locomotives to attend Doncaster works direct from the makers for inspection and acceptance, after which they would disperse to their allocated depots. Twenty of the class, D305 to D324, were built at Robert Stephenson & Hawthorn for the London Midland Region, whilst the rest were built by Vulcan Foundry. One of the RSH built engines, Crewe based D322, was the first of the class to be withdrawn in September 1967 after it received massive accident damage during a collision on the WCML. *(BLP - D7)*

55019 ROYAL HIGHLAND FUSILIER passes Hatfield & Stainforth station, with Hatfield Colliery in the background, on a Hull to King's Cross express in April 1981. Immediately north of the station was Thorne Junction where the lines to Hull and Scunthorpe diverge. South of the station was Stainforth Junction where the freight line to Thorpe Marsh power station diverged to the west. *(BLP - D45)*

55022 ROYAL SCOTS GREY heads a York to King's Cross express over the square flat crossing of the Nottingham to Lincoln route at Newark in May 1980. The ECML had four of these type of crossings between Newark and Darlington: Newark (ex Midland Railway); Tuxford (ex LD&ECR); Retford (ex Great Central); Darlington (ex North Eastern). Retford was replaced by a diveunder (*see* previous pages), and the Darlington crossing was abolished. Note the proximity of the ground level signal box. *(BLP - D66)*

Brush Type 4 D1576 nears Beaulieu Road in the New Forest with the Up *BOURNEMOUTH BELLE* Pullman in July 1967. With 3rd-rail electrification pending, and steam power on the Southern Region all but finished, this three year old, Gateshead based locomotive is being utilised on one of the region's premier workings, although the external condition of the Co-Co is far from satisfactory in the circumstances. Three Class 47's had been loaned to the Southern in September 1966 for the Bournemouth line passenger workings alongside BR Standard Cl.5's and the remaining SR Pacifics. Their main duties during that transition period included haulage of the 8.30 a.m. and 5.30 p.m. trains from Waterloo to Bournemouth, the 4.35 p.m. Waterloo to Weymouth. Return working included 12.35 p.m. and 12.59 p.m. Bourneouth to Waterloo, and the 10.13 p.m. from Weymouth. *(BLP - D31)*

Nearing Llandudno Junction, Upperby based English Electric Type 4 No.D287 heads an Up express from Holyhead to London (Euston) in June 1963. By now, these big 2,000 horsepower diesels had virtually taken over the long distance passenger workings running over the North Wales coast line, although the occasional serviceable Stanier Pacific was employed when diesel failures occurred. Nearly three years old, D287 was allocated to the Carlisle shed when it emerged new from Vulcan Foundry in August 1960. Spending all of its life working from various depots on the West Coast Main Line north of Crewe, D287, renumbered 40087 in April 1974, was based at Springs Branch diesel depot in Wigan for much of the seventies' but ended up at Longsight depot in Manchester where so many other 40's finished their working days. Withdrawn in August 1982, this locomotive was broken up at Doncaster works in October 1985. *(BLP - D30)*

The long body of the 'Peak' class locomotives can be fully appreciated in this broadside view of Derby built D35 approaching Gargrave station at the head of a Leeds (City) to Carlisle express in April 1967. *(BLP - D40)*

As an interim measure, prior to the full electrification of the West Coast Main Line north of Crewe, British Rail leased a fleet of fifty 2,700 h.p. Co-Co diesel-electric locomotives, the design of which was based on the English Electric Deltic Prototype 2 (DP2) but built instead with flat fronted ends. Numbered D400 to D449, the first of the class (by some coincidence designated Class 50 in the TOPS scheme) was released from Vulcan Foundry in September 1967 and by the end of 1968 all were in traffic and working mainly on the WCML based at Crewe. Although the first two Cl.50's had been fitted from new with external multiple unit jumper cable connections, the other forty-eight entered traffic without those fittings. However, all the internal wiring was in place in each locomotive and during 1969 BR fitted the necessary couplings and controls so that these diesels could run in pairs. This multiple running enabled the London Midland Region to accelerate the Anglo-Scottish express passenger services from mid-1970. In October 1972 Nos.400 and 401 were sent to the Western Region for trials with a view to the Class 50's eventually taking over from the WR diesel-hydraulics once electric services started between Crewe and Glasgow. On 26th June 1973 No.406, working alone and still in original livery, heads north out of Crewe with the 8.00 a.m. Euston to Glasgow (Central). *Hugh Ballantyne.*

It was March 1974 before the Western Region acquired any more of the Class 50's and during that month three of them were sent south to join the original pair. In the summer of 1975 the WCML was energised throughout and another thirty-one of the '50's' reallocated to the Western Region and over the following months the balance of the class left the LMR for the Western. During the transition period of the class from LM to WR control, BR purchased the locomotives outright knowing that they had now found an alternative to the Class 52 'Westerns'. However, reliability of the whole class dropped dramatically once on the WR with numerous factors to blame. Once these were sorted out and a refurbishment programme implemented, the class settled down to some serious work. So as not to be without their beloved 'namers', the WR decided in 1978 to name this whole class after warships of the Royal Navy. On 18th August 1979 and still in blue livery, 50035 ARK ROYAL comes around the curve from Dawlish Warren heading towards Teignmouth with the 8 10 a.m. Bristol to Penzance service. Although not quite discernible from this distance, the nameplate also has the ship's badge affixed. *Hugh Ballantyne.*

'Warship' D805 BENBOW, by now minus its nameplates, proceeds to Bath Road depot after arriving in Bristol on a freight working from the Midlands in 1972. Starting life in May 1959, D805 was released to traffic in the green livery of the period and started work from Laira shed. From 1964 it was repainted in the maroon livery which was being favoured at after the Crewe built 'Westerns'. Later, from 1966 onwards, it went to the BR blue which it wears in this view. As can be easily discerned, the bodywork, especially the all yellow painted sloping front, is looking extremely stressed but its image would hardly matter any more because in October it was condemned and Swindon, its birthplace, scrapped the locomotive during the following May. Under the BR TOPS scheme the Swindon built 'Warships' - D800 to D832 and D866 to D870 - became Class 42 whilst the North British Loco. Co. built examples, D833 to D865, became Class 43. All the 'Warships were allocated to depots for working the West of England services in the early 1960's although most members did work inter-regional passenger traffic as far north as Crewe on a daily basis. The only thing wrong with this class was the fact that they were diesel-hydraulics. Their performance with heavy trains in the West of England with its undulating route was simply superb but they were non-standard and so BR deemed that their future was bleak. Luckily a few examples have been preserved so that their compact size can be measured against their powerful performance. *Roger Griffiths.*

Yet another early diesel type which did not stand the test of time was the Beyer, Peacock built Hymek Type 3 hydraulics. Their problem was not in reliability, they were the victims of BR's decision to rid the Western Region of diesel-hydraulics in exchange for diesel-electric motive power. Admittedly they were a success in the realms of the hydraulic world of the WR but they were worked perhaps too hard and literally thrashed into submission. The few survivors which lasted to 1975 ended up in the London area. Three went into preservation whilst another three became Departmental Stock. In September 1964 a work stained two tone green liveried D7020 descends the bank into Aberystwyth with a train from Carmarthen. This particular locomotive spent much of its life working from Bath Road depot in Bristol and was on the eve of its tenth birthday when it was withdrawn in January 1972. *(BLP - D13)*

Finsbury Park 'Deltic' D9009 ALYCIDON speeds south past Eaton Wood road bridge with an Up express, IA49 for King's Cross, in June 1962. All of the London based locomotives were named after famous racehorses in the Doncaster tradition and except for D9001 ST PADDY and D9003 MELD, both named in July 1961, the others were named as they were delivered to Doncaster. *(BLP - D9)*

'Under the wires', two Class 31's headed by 31318 climb past Brookhouse sidings with a heavy coke train from Rotherwood yard to Manchester in early evening sun in September 1981. Since that date, 31318 has changed identity a couple of times; in September 1984 it became 31451 and in May 1990 it took on the number 31551, a far cry from its original 1962 number, D5852. *(BLP - D89)*

(opposite) Half way between Loughborough and Leicester, a pair of Toton's BR Sulzer Type 2's, 25258 and 25123, pass Sileby on the Midland main line with a coal train from Toton yard to London in September 1982. The signal box and semaphore bracket signals add to the typically Midland scene. Before the TOPS renumbering, 25258 had been D7608, built Derby April 1966. When new No.25123 had been D5273, another Derby build from May 1964. With the arrival of the Class 58 Co-Co diesels at Toton, and the reduction in coal traffic to London, these two locomotives both ended up at Crewe depot shortly after this scene was captured. 25123 was condemned in May 1983 and 25258 lasted until December 1984. The younger diesel (18 years) went to Swindon works for cutting up whilst the older one (19 years) was sold for scrap to Vic Berry at Leicester. *(BLP - D91)*

45

In June 1960, EE Type D243 powers a late afternoon Newcastle to King's Cross express south of Peascliffe tunnel, Grantham. Considering that most of the class found work into the 1980's, D243 (renumbered to 40043 in January 1974) was one of the few unlucky early withdrawals in January 1976. It was cut up fifteen months later at Crewe works, its last shed being Carlisle Kingmoor from where it worked mainly freight trains. *(BLP - D121)*

(opposite) An unidentified BR Derby built Sulzer Type 2 (Class 24) climbs the River Bran gorge out of Lochluichart with the morning train from Inverness to Kyle of Lochalsh in May 1974. This locomotive would have been one of the Inverness allocated batch, in the 5112 to 5132 number range, which had been associated with the Highland lines since their introduction in 1960. By the end of 1976 they had all vanished from Scotland as indeed had most of the class from BR except for a couple which hung on into 1978. Note the salmon ladder in the river. *(BLP - D34)*

Under the TOPS system the English Electric Type 4's became Class 40 with no need for any sub classes because apart from the headcode display boxes or the lack of, all the two hundred members of the class were the same. D363 had started its career at Haymarket depot in 1961 and did a lot of work on the ECML besides working northwards to Aberdeen with all sorts of traffic. In April 1974 it became 40163. During a glorious sunny afternoon in May 1981, when it was still on Haymarket's books, I caught it leading a Down ECML freight near Beningborough. In June 1982 the locomotive was withdrawn and by then it had severed its links with Edinburgh and was allocated to Longsight depot in Manchester. *(BLP - D92)*

(opposite) An unidentified Class 25 heads a train of empty ICI limestone hoppers through an autumnal landscape near Chinley in November 1982. Originally the preserve of Stanier 8F 2-8-0's, these heavy fitted trains, with their distinctive high sided bogie hoppers, plied between the ICI quarry at Tunstead near Buxton and the ICI Winnington works near Northwich, and had been worked by the Class 25's since the end of steam. *(BLP - D112)*

It is October 1981 at Hatfield & Stainforth station. In the background is Hatfield Colliery, one of the small number of working coal mines which lasted long enough to be privatised from what was left of the fast contracting British coal industry. Working its way south towards Doncaster, Class 37 No.37120 has charge of a train of empty 16-ton mineral wagons en route to another colliery where loading screens were still employed. 37120 was one of the Robert, Stephenson & Hawthorns built English Electric Type 3's which came into traffic in March 1963 numbered D6820. Initially it was allocated to Canton depot in Cardiff to work coal traffic in South Wales but a decline in production there saw it reallocated to Healey Mills depot near Wakefield. The wagons within this train were by 1981 an endangered species and by 2006 they were all but gone.*(BLP - D166)*

(opposite) Silver birch trees frame a Class 26 passing the Mossford hydroelectric generator outlet at Lochluichart with the evening train from Inverness to Kyle of Lochalsh in June 1982. *(BLP - D188)*

Brush 31156 in ex works condition, passes Charlotte Road, Sheffield with an Up train for Nottingham in April 1979. *(BLP - D144)*

(opposite) Another diesel-hydraulic class ordered by British Railways but which was not destined for the Western Region was the Yorkshire Engine Co. built 0-4-0s which first appeared in September 1960 and eventually amounted to twenty locomotives. All of these tiny locomotives were destined for work on the London Midland Region and were concentrated in Lancashire mainly in the Liverpool area although both Fleetwood shed and a couple of the Manchester depots hosted them. To carry out work which was probably the most appropriate for such a class as these, one of them was allocated to Burton-upon-Trent to help out on the brewery railways where the short wheelbase proved most useful. However, with yard shunting in rapid decline, the working days of these little diesels receded and by 1975 the class was no longer required on BR. Although some went for scrap, most went into private industrial use and from those a number have reached preservation. This is 27A Bank Hall's D2868 which is apparently standing in the yard at Shrewsbury Coleham shed in 1962. *Hugh Ballantyne collection.*

Making its way back to Thornaby depot after a general overhaul at Doncaster in April 1982, Class 37 37042 stands in the shed yard at Leeman Road, York. Already twenty years old when caught by my camera, this locomotive was one of the success stories of the Modernisation Plan. It was turned out by English Electric from Vulcan Foundry in June 1962, as D6742, and was allocated to Darnall shed before moving to Tinsley depot when that establishment opened. When renumbered in February 1974 it had been a resident of Gateshead depot for a number of years and by the end of that decade it was allocated to March depot having been at Thornaby during the interim period. It went back north to Thornaby as the 1980's dawned. However, unlike most of its kind, 37042 has never been refurbished but it is still operational (2004) and is moving freight for its new owner EWS at the grand old age of forty-two years. *(BLP - D150)*

(opposite) Two BRCW built Class 26's, with 26013 heading the Down train, meet at Garve station with west and east bound morning workings on the Inverness to Kyle of Lochalsh line in June 1976. The stationman is ready with the tablet to exchange with the crew of the Up train. The signal box, semaphore signals and road over bridge were all in place at this date but radio signalling has now replaced the old and a level crossing has taken the place of the overbridge. *(BLP - D124)*

Inverness Class 26 No.5344 (26044) climbs past the Grudie Lochan west of Lochluichart with the midday train from Inverness to Kyle of Lochalsh in June 1974. *(BLP - D39)*

(opposite) Seen from the now demolished road bridge, 26013 departs from Garve for Kyle of Lochalsh in July 1982. Formerly D5313, 26013 was one of the original BRCW Type 2's allocated to the Eastern Region at Hornsey shed in January 1959. By the summer of the following year it had migrated with the rest of the class to Scotland and went first to Haymarket depot but eventually found its way to Inverness depot from where it worked over the former Highland Railway routes which radiated from the capital of the Highlands. In September 1982 this engine went into storage from which it never emerged and it was condemned in March 1985. *(BLP - D39)*

Leeds Holbeck based Brush Co-Co D1573 heads the Up *YORKSHIRE PULLMAN* near Ordsall in June 1965. Just over a year old at the time of this picture, this Crewe built example of what became Class 47 was looking far from immaculate and its two-tone green livery is covered in rust coloured 'road dirt'. (BLP - D36)

(opposite) Class 37 37409 LOCH AWE arrives at Glenfinnan station with a Mallaig to Fort William train in July 1987. The Co-Co is in the distinctive blue livery of the period with a large logo and the Scottie dog emblem. Starting life as D6970 at Cardiff Canton depot in March 1965, this Vulcan Foundry built locomotive became 37270 in February 1974 when it was still based in South Wales, at Landore depot. It became 37409 in October 1985 and moved north to Scotland, being named during the following August. *(BLP - D154)*

Another former South Wales based Class 37 which migrated to the Highlands of Scotland was 37401, later named MARY QUEEN OF SCOTS. Seen here propelling a ballast train west of the bridge above Glenfinnan in August 1986, a dust storm has been created around the train by the spreading process of the dry ballast, a rarely photographed event, especially in this part of the world. Originally D6968, this 37 became 37268 during the first TOPS renumbering. It became 37401 in June 1985 after being completely refurbished to give it another twenty years of operational life. The name was affixed in November 1985. *(BLP - D151)*

Bampton station, Devon. Saturday, 28th September 1963. North British Loco. Co. Type 2 diesel-hydraulic D6318 draws the stock into the platform prior to working the 3.20 p.m. (Saturdays Only) service to Exeter (St Davids). Bampton was the main intermediate station on the Exe Valley branch between Tiverton and Dulverton but the branch was closed to all traffic shortly after this picture was taken. D6318's future was not that much brighter; delivered to the Western Region in March 1960, it was condemned in May 1971 and cut up at Swindon during March 1972. *Hugh Ballantyne.*

A pair of English Electric Type 1 Bo-Bo's (Class 20), headed by Toton's 20168, pass Treeton on the Up loop line in September 1981 with a long train of bolster wagons. Semaphore signals and 16-ton mineral wagons in the near sidings complete the picture. *(BLP - D140)*

55009 ALYCIDON, sporting white cab windows, leaves Newark with a York to King's Cross express in February 1981. Eleven months after this scene was captured on film the 'Deltics' were history, at least as far as British Rail was concerned. However, 55009 was purchased for preservation by the DPS. The line diverging off to the left is the freight only line to Bottesford West Junction and at its southern end it served a gypsum factory and a cement works. *(BLP - D46)*

In its one-off, almost revolutionary, desert sand livery the first 'Western' diesel-hydraulic D1000 WESTERN ENTERPRISE leaves Shrewsbury and makes toward Crewe with a train from the West of England bound for the north-west in 1962. Note also the lack of a yellow warning panel on the front. This unique livery did not stay with the locomotive throughout its life, as from about 1967 it became one of the BR 'corporate' blue examples along with the rest of the class. Besides this livery, various members of the class were turned out in green, maroon, blue and another one-off colour - Golden Ochre - as worn by D1015 WESTERN CHAMPION from new in January 1963. *Hugh Ballantyne collection.*

One of Tinsley depots' numerous Class 47's, 47310, pulls slowly away from Treeton Colliery on the Up loop line with a heavy merry-go-round coal train in May 1980. Class 25 No.25293, seen earlier, is ticking over in the foreground whilst awaiting a signal. Treeton signal box and the fine array of semaphores make a glorious scene before the final commissioning of colour light signalling, under Sheffield power box, changed the area for ever. *(BLP - D141)*

Refurbished '37' 37406 THE SALTIRE SOCIETY passes the islands at the west end of Loch Eilt with a Fort William to Mallaig train in June 1987. Previous identities for this locomotive were D6995 as built in July 1965, then 37295 from May 1974. It became 37406 from August 1985 and in June the following year gained its nameplates. *(BLP - D117)*

On a dull, cold Saturday 24th March 1979, Class 27 No.27203 is leaving Edinburgh Waverley and is bound for Glasgow (Queen Street) on one of the recently introduced regular interval shuttle services. These trains were 'top and tailed' at the time and, not visible, 27106 was at the rear of this formation. *Hugh Ballantyne.*

37407 carries the more appropriate name LOCH LONG and is passing the west end of the Dubh Loch (Deep or Black Loch) with the late afternoon Fort William to Mallaig train in July 1987. This '37' (D6605 until March 1974) was amongst the last batch of EE Type 3's to be built - D6600 to D6608 - and their numbers preceded the original three hundred which had gone before them. However, once again we must ask the question about this last batch - why nine? Why not ten? *(BLP - D107)*

Introduced on the last day of May 1960, the *ANGLO SCOTTISH CAR CARRIER* service started its short life being steam hauled but by June 1963 the diesels had taken over and save the odd failure, steam was never to head this train again on a regular basis. Approaching Grantham with the Up service in the late afternoon of a June day in 1963, York based English Electric Type 4 D354 displays the central headcode fitted to the latter members (D345-D399) of this 200-strong class. Built at Vulcan foundry, D354 came into service during July 1961. Withdrawn in January 1982, it languished at Healey Mills yard for some time before being towed to Swindon works where, in November 1985, it was cut up. *(BLP - D15)*

BR Class 25 25293, one of the Beyer, Peacock built batch (works No.8053) from February 1966, nears Treeton North junction with a Down ballast train in April 1980. Originally D7643, and allocated to Sheffield Tinsley depot when new, it moved onto the London Midland lines before it was renumbered in February 1974. Withdrawn in February 1981, it was scrapped at Swindon works in during the following August. *(BLP - D48)*

D9010 passes Ordsall with the Up *TEES-TYNE PULLMAN* in April 1962. This train seems to have been a regular turn for the Haymarket based 'Deltics'. *(BLP - D11)*

45120 (D107) emerges from the west end of Standedge tunnel with a York to Liverpool express amid an autumnal landscape in October 1982. The infant River Tame which with the Goyt become the Mersey at Stockport, passes beneath the track just in front of the tunnel mouth. Just out of picture to the right, are the two single bores of the now disused first and second tunnels. Withdrawn in March 1987 after nearly twenty-seven years of faithful service, 45120 ended up in the closed Tinsley yard with dozens of its class mates awaiting the scrap merchants. *(BLP - D129)*

Approaching Fairwood Junction with an Up West of England express, an unidentified 'Western' looks almost brand-new in 1975. By now a number of the class had already been withdrawn and more than a dozen had been cut up at Swindon works. However, this particular locomotive has highly polished body sides and looks anything other than ready for scrap. The maroon paint used by Crewe works and which adorned many of the class prior to Chromatic blue becoming standard after 1967, was reputedly the same paint as applied to the London Midland Stanier Pacifics. *Roger Griffiths.*

On a warn September evening in 1981, 'Peak' 45075 (D132) passes Whittington with a Down freightliner train. The semaphore signal gantry and the signal box were still in use at the old station platform. *(BLP - D44)*

45122 (D11) passes Foxlow Junction signal box with a Down early morning freight in August 1981. The box and the semaphore signals were still in use on the old layout, but all that changed when colour lights were introduced. The track leading off to the left went to various collieries in the area such as Bolsover and Markham before reaching the Worksop-Mansfield line at Creswell. *(BLP - D75)*

The view from the other side of Foxlow Junction gives a good vista of the Staveley Iron and Chemical works in the distant background. 45007 (D119) passes with a Down ballast train on a warm July evening in 1986. Note that the signal box and semaphore signals are hanging on. *(BLP - D105)*

With its green paintwork looking past its best, six-year old 'Peak' D34 heads north past Garsdale with a Carlisle bound express in July 1967. *(BLP - D38)*

Remember GT3, the English Electric gas-turbine prototype built at Vulcan Foundry and released for trials in 1961? Here it is at Whitchurch in March 1961 being shunted into the former engine shed yard by 'Peak' D10 TRYFAN, after having failed during a test run between Crewe and Shrewsbury. The engine shed became its base during the various road tests it undertook prior to its official unveiling at the Institute of Locomotive Engineers exhibition held at Marylebone on 12th May. It was still early days for the 4-6-0 tender engine and it was not officially loaned to British Railways by its makers until after the London exhibition. From then until it was withdrawn in October 1962, the prototype proved time and again that it had the power to haul a heavy passenger train at speed over the West Coast Main Line between Crewe and Carlisle. Even Shap was overcome without too much difficulty but the locomotive was a one-off and having already invested millions of pounds in diesel-electric traction, BR could not afford to invest in a fleet of gas-turbine motive power no matter how good the prototype may have performed. Returned to Newton-le-Willows, GT3 was stripped of the power unit and the sold as scrap to a merchant in Brindle Heath, Salford. *Hugh Ballantyne.*

Hauling a King's Cross bound express, 55016 GORDON HIGHLANDER nears Retford station and is passing the old Great Northern goods shed in May 1981. Another December 1981 withdrawal, this locomotives was lucky enough to be chosen for preservation by the D9000 Fund. *(BLP - D93)*

Keeping company with Liddel Water on its way to Hawick, Haymarket based BRCW Type 2 D5307, in its original green livery, climbs out of Newcastleton with a Carlisle to Edinburgh (Waverley) train in June 1965. Already nearly seven years old, this engine started life at Hornsey shed and finished it in January 1977 at Inverness depot. *(BLP - D199)*

Class 37 37418 rounds the curve by Mossford hydro-electric power station, Lochluichart with the evening train from Inverness to Kyle of Lochalsh in June 1986. Three months later this '37' was also named - An Comunn Gaidhealach - joining the growing band of locomotives carrying a legend which was certainly not English in origin. *(BLP - D132)*

EE Type 4 D286 became Class 40 No.40086 in March 1974 but the blue livery was applied some years before that. In July 1984, with less than six months of its life left, it passes the bracket signal at Edale whilst working an evening parcels train through the Hope Valley to Manchester. Having started life in July 1960 working from Gateshead depot, this Type 4 worked out the last years of its life allocated, like many of its kin, to Longsight. Within weeks of withdrawal the locomotive was cut up at Doncaster works. *(BLP - D106)*

Diverted because of Sunday engineering work on its usual route via Dronfield, 45142 (D83) takes an Up main line express from Sheffield over the freight only route towards Staveley and is passing Foxlow Junction with its bracket semaphore signals in April 1980. Note the track rationalisation taking place. *(BLP - D49)*

A smart looking Longsight based Class 40, No.40117 (D317), works a Down ballast train at Treeton South Junction in April 1980. This '40' has probably brought this load of ballast from the Buxton area. Note the Class 20 on the right waiting for a signal. *(BLP - D47)*

A month later, same location, another Class 20 awaits the road as 'Peak' 46021 (D158) passes beneath the semaphore bracket signals with a Down steel coil empties train. Because of the sharp decline in freight traffic during 1980, the Plymouth Laira based '46' was put into store five months later and then withdrawn shortly afterwards. However, it was reinstated in November 1981 for a fourteen-month long second life working mainly from Gateshead depot. It was cut up at Swindon works in June 1985. *(BLP - D65)*

37261 CAITHNESS rounds the curve at Attadale Bay with an Inverness to Kyle of Lochalsh train in September 1985. *(BLP - D171)*

Of all the TOPS locomotive renumbering which took place between 1973 and 1975, the most untidy batch of renumbering concerned the 'Peaks', or at least those which became Class 45. The Class 46 - D138 to D193 became 46001 to 46056 in that order - perfect. Whoever sanctioned the random renumbering of D11 to D137 must have been having sleepless nights or perhaps were on a medication which induced chaos. The class ended up numbered 45001 to 45077, and 45101 to 45150. Anyway, 'Peak' 45127, formerly D87, leaves Mossley behind as it climbs the steady gradient towards Standedge with a Liverpool to Hull express in July 1984. (BLP - D88)

With track rationalisation evident all around it, 'Deltic' 55010 THE KING'S OWN SCOTTISH BORDERER, now wearing the all over blue livery, departs Doncaster and is passing Hexthorpe bridge with a York to King's Cross express in July 1981. This engine gained its regimental name in May 1965. By now the Deltic's were nearing the end of their lives and six of the class had already been withdrawn with four of those cut up at Doncaster works. 55010's turn came in December 1981 and it was cut up at Doncaster during the following May. *(BLP - D120)*

D5 CROSS FELL, another of the 2,300 h.p. 'Peaks', shows off its near 68 foot length at Toton in May 1970. When withdrawn from their short sojourn in main line passenger service, D1 to D10 had their steam heating boilers removed which effectively sealed their fate to freight service only. During their time at Toton, it was usual to see these locomotives hauling coal trains to public utilities and rail centres. Although in a clean condition, the paintwork of the '44' has suffered from too many trips through the washing plant. Two of the original 'Peaks', D4 GREAT GABLE and D8 PENYGHENT have managed to reach preservation but the two featured on these pages were cut up at Derby works, D1 in February 1977 and D5 in December 1978. *(BLP - D60)*

55021 ARGYLL AND SUTHERLAND HIGHLANDER passes the site of Dukeries Junction, Tuxford with a morning express from York to King's Cross in May 1980. *(BLP - D84)*

55008 THE GREEN HOWARDS nears York North with an Up express from Newcastle in May 1981. Whereas most of the class had their headcode panels painted yellow, 55008's panel was black with the two white discs. *(BLP - D63)*

Unlike their steam locomotive forebears, diesel locomotives have a habit of being named one minute and then being stripped of the legend/title the next. There are also cases of the same name being passed from one locomotive to another in the same class. Class 37 37260 RADIO HIGHLAND, ex works in blue livery with the large logo in July 1984, was one such diesel although circumstances dictated the removal of the name. Having been named just a few days before I caught it on film, it lost the name in September 1989 when it was condemned at Doncaster. The name was then passed on to 37113. Here in August 1984, an immaculate 37260 passes the Grudie Lochan west of Lochluichart with the mid-day Inverness to Kyle of Lochalsh train in August 1984. *(BLP - D97)*

45112 (D61) departs from Chesterfield with a morning local train from Nottingham to Sheffield in June 1986. The crooked church spire dominates the town backdrop. This locomotive was bestowed the name ROYAL ARMY ORDNANCE CORPS in September 1965 but somewhere along the way the plates had been removed. In May 1987 this 'Peak' was withdrawn and dumped with other '45's' in the former marshalling yard at March in Cambridgeshire. *(BLP - D108)*

In a scene which could be described as the natural environment of the class, 'Peak' 45146 (D66) heads south along the Erewash Valley line near North Wingfield with a Sheffield to St.Pancras, via Nottingham, express in September 1981. The original Midland four track semaphore controlled formation has given way to this all too familiar Up and Down colour light rationalised 'speedway' with few, if any, crossovers, sidings or junctions. When the 'Peaks' first came into traffic in the early 1960's they would have been passing this spot at the rate of five or six every hour, in between the steam hauled coal, coke, steel and general goods trains which monopolised the route - happy days indeed. *(BLP - D77)*

Class 24 No.5140 is working a goods train, comprised mainly of hopper wagons, along the North Staffordshire branch from Stoke-on-Trent to Leek Brook Junction on 23rd March 1973 and is passing the remains of the station at Stockton Brook, which closed in May 1956 when the line lost its passenger service. Since then, limited freight services hauling stone from Caldon Low and Oakamoor ran until 1988 but the line has since become dormant although the track is still in situ. The Derby built Sulzer Bo-Bo was one of ten delivered new to Longsight depot during October and November 1960. It finished its working days In January 1976 whilst allocated to Crewe diesel depot. Nine months later it was cut up at Swindon. *Hugh Ballantyne.*

Last word to a Deltic - 55007 PINZA passes a virtually empty Dringhouses yard whilst en route to Leeds with a Newcastle to Liverpool express in September 1981. *(BLP - D69)*